AF255895

My Mommy's A Trucker

by: Robyn Mitchell
art by: Douglas Brown

Claire looked through the window and saw Mommy's big red truck.

"Look Daddy, Mommy is here to take me with her in the big red truck."

Claire and her daddy stood at the door and watched as her mommy climbed down the steps of the big truck.

Claire jumped into her mommy's arms. "Oh Mommy, today is going to be so much fun, riding in your big red truck."

Mommy hugged Claire.

Claire and her mommy walked
down the sidewalk.

They turned and waved at her daddy
who stood in the doorway.

Daddy waved back. "Drive safe and be careful.
I will see you tonight for dinner."

"Come on, Claire." Mommy pointed to the load of
lumber. Claire's mommy drove a Flatbed Trailer.

"Today you will help me deliver that lumber
to the lumberyard. Are you ready?"
"Oh, yes, Mommy." Claire giggled.

Mommy opened the passenger side door
of the big red truck.

Claire climbed up the steps and into the car sea
that her mommy had placed in the passenger
seat of the cab.

Mommy secured Claire with
a click of the seatbelt.

Mommy sat in the driver's seat and secured her own seatbelt. "Now we are ready to go to work in the big red truck."

Claire watched Mommy push down on the pedals near her feet. She moved the long stick that was between the seats.

Mommy pushed in on two big buttons on the
dashboard. "SHH!" the big red truck said.

Mirrors were attached to the doors
on each side of the big red truck.
Mommy moved her head from side to side,
looked at the mirrors on the doors.
"All clear," Mommy said.

The big red truck moved from the driveway
onto the street.

Claire looked through the big windshield
of the big red truck. "I can see everything
from way up here."

On the highway, Claire spotted a big green truck going in the opposite direction.

Claire pointed at the big green truck. "Look Mommy, another big truck. Why does its trailer look like a box?

"There are all types of trailers.
That one is called a Box Trailer."

"I drive a Flatbed Trailer."
Mommy said with a smile.

A trailer with a picture of a cow rolled by them. Mommy pointed at it. "That big cylinder is a Tanker Trailer; they deliver milk and water."

14

Soon Claire spotted another truck and trailer. "Look at that trailer Mommy, it has a big tractor on it." "That's a Low-Boy Trailer. Those carry really big things." Mommy stated.

For the next few miles they played a game, as they tried to spot as many different trailers as they could along the highway.

"Let's play another game," said Mommy. "Let's look for different traffic signs."
"Okay." Claire pointed to a black and white sign with a 55 on it. "What is that one for?"

Mommy smiled. "That is a speed sign that tells me how fast I can go on the road. On this road, I can only go 55 miles an hour."

A green sign with white letters appeared and
Claire called out, "Exit 126, one mile."

"Good, Claire. Exit 126 goes to the lumberyard."
She moved a stick on her steering wheel and
the right turn signal blinked.

Mommy pushed the pedals and then shifted
the stick in the middle of the cab.

The big red truck began to slow down.
They moved down the exit ramp
and stopped at the intersection.

"I know what that red sign is—it is a stop sign."

"That's right. Good for you, Claire."

Mommy moved the stick and the steering wheel
again and the left signal blinked.
When the intersection was clear, Mommy turned
the big red truck onto a two-lane road.

Smoke huffed and puffed from the tall silver
stacks as the big red truck went faster.

Claire spotted a small green and white street sign
on a pole and read: "Lumber Yard Road."

"That road sign tells us we are on the right road,"
Mommy explained.
"And we live on Circle Street. I've seen that sign
at the end of our road." Claire replied.

22

The big red truck turned into the parking lot of a lumber store. "Do you see that sign with the arrows?" Mommy asked.

"It has lots of words. What does it say?" Claire asked. "All deliveries must go to the back of the building." Mommy explained.

Mommy slowly moved the big red truck behind the lumber store. There were rows of open doors high off the ground.
"What are those?" Claire asked.

"Those are loading docks. I can back the flatbed trailer to one so the workers can take the lumber. The big red truck went, "beep, beep, beep," as Mommy backed it up to the dock.

A man came out of a side door and climbed on
the step on the driver's side door.

Mommy rolled down the window and
handed him a piece of paper.

The man took the paper and talked into a little
black box on his shoulder.

Small yellow vehicles with spikes on the front of
them rolled onto the dock. "What are those,
Mommy?" "Those are forklifts. The men on the
dock will use them to take the lumber off
Mommy's trailer." Mommy replied.

Claire watched as several people removed the
straps that held down the large bundles
of lumber. Then the forklifts came and
picked up the lumber.

Claire waved good-bye to the men on the dock.

"When we get home, I'm going to tell Daddy all about the forklift, the dock, and the workers. And, I'm going to draw pictures of all the signs we saw today."

SPEED SIGN

EXIT SIGN

STOP SIGN

STREET SIGN

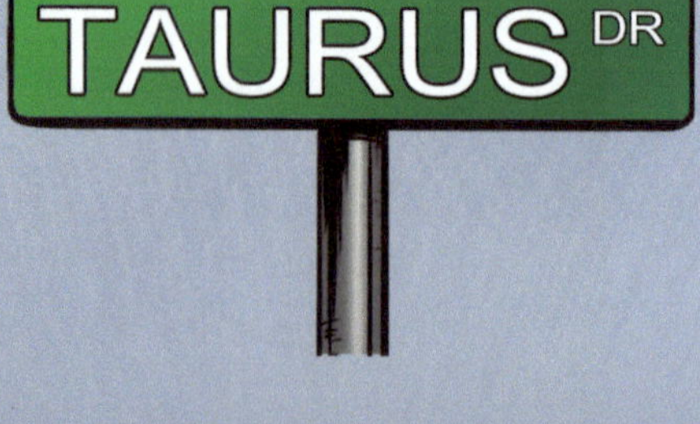

28

"And, all the different trailers we saw today."

"And, I'm going to draw a picture of us
riding in your big red truck."

"Someday I'm going to drive a big red truck,
just like you, Mommy."